Dead End Road

E.C. Hanson

Copyright 2024 E.C. Hanson

All rights reserved. No part of this book may be reproduced in any form without permission from the author or publisher, except as permitted by U.S. copyright law.

To request permission, contact E.C. Hanson (erikhanson2121@gmail.com) or AnuciPress (tanuci69@gmail.com).

Cover by Alexis Macaluso

ISBN: 979-8-9919612-3-3 (print)

ISBN: 979-8-9919612-4-0 (Ebook)

First Edition 2024 by Anuci Press

anuci-press.com

DEAD END ROAD

By E.C. Hanson

AUTHOR'S NOTE

Could you classify what you're about to read as an actual true crime book? Well, it deals with a real murder. But it also hones in on how I became involved, so maybe it is more like a true crime memoir. Since the case is still active, I had to sift through whatever articles were available and speak with as many people as I could who remember the crime. As you read, you will be reminded that I am not a detective, private investigator, or reporter. I'm just a dude who watches a lot of *Dateline* and one who learned about this case in March of 2024. I used this example on The Lisa Wexler Show, so forgive me if you're one of the few who already heard it. Someone said solving this case would be like a marathon. But I view it as a relay race.

While there are a fixed number of members on relay teams, the number of teammates for this case depends on how many become interested and choose to do something to get justice for Renee Freer. I start by writing a book. That next teammate will take my book, process what's relevant, discard what's not (which, truth be told, might be significantly larger than what's relevant), and create a podcast. Once this person makes the next handoff, a person will create a TikTok and play the role of social media sleuth. The final person will get it on *Dateline* or *Unsolved Mysteries*. The result of everyone's collective efforts?

A solved case.

For Ken Heim

Prologue

I was in the woods.

On the eve of summer.

I only had one more day of third grade left.

I went next door to see if my friend Bonnie was available.

She wasn't.

I had to improvise.

I searched for someone to play with. One person I knew well made themselves available. They led me to the woods. I followed their lead because I trusted them.

I didn't want the evening to end, but I knew there would be two months' worth of nights like this one.

The sky darkened, informing me that I would have to get home soon. But my mother didn't call out my name (like she was wont to do), so I took advantage of the extra minutes and vanished into the joy of this moment.

For a reason unbeknownst to me, this familiar person tried to rip my shirt off. I tried to get away. But then I felt something hit my head.

What could I have done to deserve that? Just because I didn't want to get raped?

Before I developed an answer to the question, this familiar figure, and someone I called a friend, smashed my skull a second time with a stone bigger than my head.

I knew my life was ending and wondered if my mother would get back home and find me in time.

My brain said no, but my heart begged for it to be a reality so I could share one last moment with my mother and my younger brother Nathaniel, the one everybody called Deeky.

I felt someone drag my body to a random spot to keep it out of sight.

I couldn't believe they were about to abandon me.

I couldn't believe I would miss the last day of school.

I couldn't believe I would never see Abby, Kerri, or Tawny again.

I died on June 22, 1977.

My name was Renee Freer.

I was 8 years old.

As of October 2024, my case was still unsolved.

SUSPICIOUS MINDS

I stared at a Facebook message sent to someone who was apparently very close to Renee Freer. It still showed SENT instead of SEEN, so I wanted to give this individual the benefit of the doubt and allow them a grace period. That said, I knew they knew I reached out to them, so I wondered: *If this person was as close to Renee as had been advertised, why hadn't this person replied to me? Why hadn't this person wished me luck and tried to recruit more members for the Facebook group to get justice for their friend? Why hadn't they told me to fuck off for writing a secondhand account about an event they wanted to clear from their memory bank?*

I sent the message on May 2nd. It was now October 23rd.

I closed my aging laptop (Condition: Replace Soon) and hoped like hell that this person would communicate with me at some point. But the more silence I received, the more suspicious I became.

GOOGLE EARTH

Early in my research process, someone provided the name of one of the principal persons of interest (because you can't refer to them as suspects anymore). After finding that the possible killer had a profile on Facebook, I visited their page and stared at their profile picture. I asked, "Could you have done it? Could your young self (around thirteen, give or take a year or two) have bashed Renee Freer's face in with a stone?"

I didn't want the person's intense face to dictate my opinion. I had to remain neutral. Just because they were one of the first names I heard didn't mean anything.

I contacted my secret weapon, a researcher with a knack for unearthing information in seconds. Shortly thereafter, they provided the address of the person I was staring at.

I punched in their current address on Google Earth, and a modest house came up. A few vehicles were in the cracked driveway. A person stood near the vehicle furthest from view. They stared at the camera as if they were staring right at me or anyone else who dared to search their address.

It was eerie.

Had the Google Earth squad put the potential murderer in the shot on purpose? Or was it just a bizarre coincidence?

RUNAWAY TRAIN

The Facebook group I created called WHO KILLED RENEE FREER was getting out of goddamn control. After an article in The Monroe Sun, CT Post, and a segment on Channel 12 News Connecticut, the number of members jumped from 58 to over 320.

Fox 61, NBC Connecticut, WTNH, and New York Daily News snagged it. Melissa in the Morning and a radio station with a million followers aired a quick segment.

Members posted wild theories, and some posted beautiful memories about Renee Freer. A few people created anonymous accounts and named persons of interest without context. Others came forward with information yet refused to go to the police, which enraged me to no end. Here was a mathematical formula that would never fail:

Wanting justice for Renee + Not speaking up on her behalf ≠ Justice for Renee

My writer buddy warned me that a Facebook group could get out of control. It was heading in that direction, but it brought so much newfound exposure to Renee Freer's active case that I had to swallow the good and the bad. Despite that fact, I wrote a message asking group members to help prevent the forum from turning into Reddit, and then I posted it.

I wanted to push the powers that be to solve this case while I wrote a book about how I grew up in a town without ever hearing about this horrific murder.

Never as a cautionary tale.

Nothing.

Had I heard about this crime at an early age, I might have done very little. But I still would have asked adults to drum up some interest because more needed to be written about it.

No annual reminders in the Monroe Courier or The Connecticut Post (formerly The Bridgeport Post).

Had the cops wanted it that way? Had the townsfolk of Monroe pretended that such a sickening tragedy didn't happen in their peaceful community? Had they all agreed to keep this one out of the conversation?

If true, a part of me couldn't blame them.

Who wants to chat about the grisly murder of a young girl?

Not I, and I was born a year after the murder took place!

I thought about people in the Facebook group that I could turn into administrators so I could be left alone to write my book. That was all I desired. But then I received a new message with a lead.

Then another.

And another.

And another.

And another.

Most messages led to nothing. But some caught my eye and caused me to sit up. I didn't want the members to trust me, though; I wanted them to trust the police.

Would people come forward with bits of information and never tell anyone else? It was certainly tracking that way.

For someone who hated humans yet believed in humanity, I had to ask myself: *How on earth did I get here?*

How?

THE BEGINNING

I had become hyperaware of my mortality. The second toe on my left foot hurt every time I put pressure on it. I started to have a burning sensation in my right leg. I wondered if my habit of consuming two big beers and a glass of whiskey nightly (sorry, doctors!) was the cause of all this or if I, acting invincible until this point, had officially become old at the ripe age of 45. Since my mother had a debilitating disease, I felt like I needed to do something, not necessarily something to get my ass killed but something with purpose before the cancer, heart attack, stroke, aneurism, or dementia came knocking. It's the one thing my brother and friends agreed on: Give a man a purpose, and you give him life.

After getting accepted into UMass Lowell's Criminal Justice program, the questions started about what I intended to do with such a degree if I could secure the loans and work it out with my busy schedule. Friends and family tossed out the career options as if they were the ones who were considering this new path, but all I could think about was writing a true crime book someday.

I had no clue what this path would entail or how I would gain access to information to cases that intrigued me. But on a work break, I Googled "unsolved murder cases in Monroe, Connecticut."

A Facebook link for *The Forgotten Cases* came up. A majority of the screen was black. But there was a tiny and unclear pic of a cute girl with pigtails in the middle of the page. She immediately reminded me of Pippi Longstocking, the fictional main character created by Swedish author Astrid Lindgren. But cuter. More innocent. Less annoying. My eyes traveled to the right of the screen, which presented the following text: *On June 22, 1977, eight-year-old Renee Freer left her home on Williams Drive in Monroe at 6 pm that evening to visit a friend whose house was just up the street. When she didn't return, a relative started to look for her. Not finding her, the relative called the police at 9:15 pm. Her lifeless body was found at 10:12 pm that evening, about 300 yards from her house near Hattertown Road. The young girl from Monroe, CT, had been bludgeoned to death, and a large stone was found nearby. She had last been seen wearing a blouse and shorts. When her body was discovered, the collar of the blouse was found slightly torn. To this date, no one has been charged with this horrendous crime. There is a $50,000 dollar reward being offered in this criminal case.*

I kept my composure because my students were in the classroom with me. But the fact that a murder happened in my hometown and I nor my friends had ever heard about it was downright shocking. I had spent endless hours outside as a kid in the 80s. How had this not been a cautionary tale for kids?

Come home before it's dark.
You don't know what kind of creeps are out there.
Remember what happened to the Freer girl?

But this murder case wasn't a part of Monroe's lore, and it unnerved me. I froze as I continued to read the rest of the passage. *If you have any information about this brutal crime, please call Detective Heim at the Monroe Police Department at 203-261-3622.*

Detective Heim?!

Ken Heim?!

My former stepfather.

Whether I was going to write anything about the Renee Freer murder, one thing was immediately obvious: I had to figure out what Ken Heim knew about it.

EX-STEPSISTER #1

I contacted my ex-stepsister. I did all this after contacting my ex-stepfather's wife because I couldn't find his number or email online. His Facebook profile was blank, too.

I hadn't seen or spoken to the ex-stepsister mentioned above in over thirty years, but I felt compelled to reach out since Ken, my ex-stepfather, was retired.

I prayed he was still alive.

It only took her a few hours to respond to my Facebook message. Her response was as follows:

Hello! Great to hear from you. Family is doing well! It's funny that you messaged me today cause I was coming to see my Dad. I gave him the message and wrote down all of your information. He is not on Facebook. My stepmom has been on medical leave from her job right now so that's probably why she didn't get your message yet. Seems like you are doing great things with writing and the jobs. Keep it up. Great hearing from you!

I wanted to write back and tell her that nothing was great about the writing or the jobs, but I refrained. She didn't need to know that I sucked at life.

Since she told Ken to contact me, I kept refreshing my email. But my workday passed. Shortly after I got home, my phone lit up with a somewhat familiar number. I kept repeating the digits in my head until it finally clicked: It was my ex-stepfather's home number.

A phone chat? Crap. I didn't want a phone chat. Nothing against Ken, but I preferred to fire off my questions via email, wish him well, and then cruise through my criminal justice program at whatever pace I could handle.

I played the message; his slow and choppy voice triggered me. Part of me wondered how his drawl aided him during questioning suspects over the years.

"*Hi, Erik. This is Ken, your ex-stepfather. Give me a call. I don't go on Facebook or anything like that. All I have is my computer.*" He provided his phone number and said, "*It never changed. Okay, take care.*"

Since his wife was on medical leave, I pondered when I should call back and thought about what I could ask him. *How have you been? How's your health, buddy? Is it better not to be married to my mom? Do you want to work on a cold case together? How about the unsolved one about Renee Freer?* The last two questions spun through my mind constantly, as if I, an educator and writer, would get an immediate invite to quench my thirst for justice.

I considered calling from my workplace since it was MCAS (Massachusetts Comprehensive Assessment System) day. As an Academic Coordinator, I didn't have to test any students. Therefore, I could get full periods where no students were in my room. But the guilt sank in that I would get paid while I chatted with Ken about topics that interested me. Instead of milking the clock by talking with him, I milked the clock by continuing my read of Katherine Ramsland's *Confession of a Serial Killer: The Untold Story of Dennis Rader – The BTK Killer*.

THE LONG AND SHORT OF IT

Renee Freer's mother was dead. Witnesses were dead. Some of the detectives who worked the case were dead. What was the point of going down this road? Was I a fool? An attention-seeking fool?

I considered all the questions and mentally reviewed what was available about Renee's case on the Internet and social media.

Jack shit.

There was nothing on social media—no Facebook groups for Renee. No TikTok sleuths spitting out theories about what happened to her. Why was this one quiet for so long?

I knew I had to get involved beyond attempting a book. Even if my book were total shit, it would exist as a document, an exposure tool, about Renee's unsolved case. The true crime professionals could take over afterward, dredge up the whole town for information I wasn't able to secure, and then put this case in the solved file.

SEEKING ANSWERS VIA EMAIL

Ken,

Thanks for taking the time to talk with me today. It was nice to reconnect. And if anything I ask below is a no-go, reject me. I respect your feelings and the emotions that come from an unsolved case. I'm pro-cops/detectives! While I know that I will reach out with more questions, here are a few on my mind:

-Would the Chief of Police or current detective on the Freer case chat with me on the phone or in person? Would I be able to view any docs from the Freer investigation? Get specific details? *The articles online are few and far between.

-Would you be okay with me writing something about this particular case? It could be an essay, article, or a short book. I have ties to the publishing world and an editor who has written two popular true crime books.

THE LONG AND SHORT OF IT

Renee Freer's mother was dead. Witnesses were dead. Some of the detectives who worked the case were dead. What was the point of going down this road? Was I a fool? An attention-seeking fool?

I considered all the questions and mentally reviewed what was available about Renee's case on the Internet and social media.

Jack shit.

There was nothing on social media—no Facebook groups for Renee. No TikTok sleuths spitting out theories about what happened to her. Why was this one quiet for so long?

I knew I had to get involved beyond attempting a book. Even if my book were total shit, it would exist as a document, an exposure tool, about Renee's unsolved case. The true crime professionals could take over afterward, dredge up the whole town for information I wasn't able to secure, and then put this case in the solved file.

SEEKING ANSWERS VIA EMAIL

Ken,

Thanks for taking the time to talk with me today. It was nice to reconnect. And if anything I ask below is a no-go, reject me. I respect your feelings and the emotions that come from an unsolved case. I'm pro-cops/detectives! While I know that I will reach out with more questions, here are a few on my mind:

-*Would the Chief of Police or current detective on the Freer case chat with me on the phone or in person? Would I be able to view any docs from the Freer investigation? Get specific details? *The articles online are few and far between.*

-*Would you be okay with me writing something about this particular case? It could be an essay, article, or a short book. I have ties to the publishing world and an editor who has written two popular true crime books.*

-How often do the cops speak with the primary suspect? Is he a local? Can you share his name? Do they monitor his daily activity? What is his general attitude? Think there is any way to bait him into confessing?

And, lastly, on a different note...

-How would I get criminal records about my father in CT and Oregon? I think he was arrested in both states. Perhaps there were a few more.

*It is okay with me if you don't answer ALL these questions. We can find a day in the future to chat in person at a diner or coffee shop. But if I can help you and the department in any way, I will try to contribute...something.

Have a great week, Ken. Thanks for everything.

Ken called me back and said, "I can't tell you nothing about the Freer case." However, he shared that he might be able to assist in getting information about my father. His response deflated me. At that moment, I realized I didn't care to learn about the specifics of my father's troubles with the law; I mostly knew them. I desperately wanted to discuss Renee Freer and determine why the case mattered so much to him. I could tell by the tenor in his voice that it was tough to discuss. Instead of pressing the issue, I hung on the line while we talked about our families. I closed my eyes and pretended I was living in his log cabin again.

The log cabin my mother hated.

THE SRO GUY

I returned to work after the Easter holiday (which was no holiday to me) and walked past the School Resource Officer. Rather brazenly, I asked him to meet me in my classroom because I wanted to learn more about FOIA (the Freedom of Information Act) requests. I knew that he spent most of his time with a therapy dog, but I felt he could steer me in the right direction. He showed up to my classroom a few minutes later. I shouldn't have invited him, though; the dude had a major case of laryngitis.

Despite his weak and raspy voice, the officer thought I would have no trouble getting the FOIA but suggested I sell myself as a writer instead of the former stepson of a guy who worked the case. I took the officer's advice and submitted a FOIA request to the state of Connecticut. My message was short, sweet, and right to the point. I expected to get exactly what I wanted soon.

Since multiple students were absent during my Period 1 session, I drank kombucha and printed up the only articles about Renee Freer I could find. The result? A scant discovery of three tiny write-ups. Why so little after forty-seven years? I couldn't write much of anything with this amount of information. Nobody could.

Frustrated by the minimal attention on Renee's case over the years, I sent emails to various newspapers in Connecticut. I stressed that I wasn't seeking attention. Quite the contrary, I wanted justice for Renee, and I believed that it was high time that someone, at the very goddamn least, wrote a new article about her.

I assumed I would get replies straight away. When that didn't happen, I opened up the latest book I checked out from the library: *Unmasked: My Life Solving America's Cold Cases*. The book's back cover was a full-body shot of the detective. No book summary. No blurbs. No publication details. Only a barcode and this broad Caucasian dude standing in the weeds in front of what looked like a dilapidated house. I wondered if the publisher had to fight him about putting the barcode there. Regardless, I couldn't wait to read this one. It's worth sharing that I sent the author a message on IG. I expected no reply. But if cold cases were his bag, I thought who better than him to help me get justice for Renee Freer.

Students showed up while I daydreamed about smoking out the main person of interest in the case. My first student couldn't find the bathroom pass, which usually dangled from my pencil sharpener. It wasn't there, which meant someone stole it. I conveyed my frustration with a sigh and convinced him to take a small spaceship-looking device that, from what I was told, hid earbuds.

Moments after the student departed, I received an email about my FOIA request:

No records or information responsive to your request were identified. Please reach out to the Town of Monroe Police Department Records Unit at (203) 452-2800. You can also file a records request with them using the website below.

I clicked on the link—error message. I opened Safari and tried again. Still nothing. I nearly snapped and tossed my school computer on the floor, but my student returned so I smiled at him and pretended everything was A-OK.

THE EARLY ARTICLES

I reviewed all the information I had access to about Renee Freer and realized it added up to very little. There was a page on Facebook called *The Forgotten Cases*, where I found my former stepfather's name. Somebody posted it on June 17, 2013. Being reconnected with Ken Heim felt even more cosmic since he had been retired for six years by then. Therefore, whoever posted this assumed he was still the point person. Good intentions for them; happy accident for me.

Next, there was a website called *Savagewatch*. It was devoted to "unsolved murders, crime, treasure, and the paranormal." At the top of the main page were icons that listed cases for each state. As I scrolled through the cases for Connecticut, I stopped when I found a tiny picture of Renee Freer (the same one from the Facebook page) with a headline in bold, black print: **Innocence Stolen Forever**. This was, more or less, the exact text listed on the Facebook page. The one difference, however, was the point of contact.

Was this Lieutenant still on the force? I made a note to find out.

I contacted Terry Sutton and asked him about the site. He explained how his intentions for the site changed over time: "Decided it was better to focus on unsolved crime. Started in Connecticut and branched off to other states in New England and beyond." He continued, emphasizing the importance of keeping the heat on the powers that be. "Community puts pressure on police and states and district's attorneys to spend more time on certain cases. Some detectives are awesome at their jobs while others are not."

After agreeing with every word of his rationale, I cruised to a blog called *Count Every Mystery* that proudly announced it was "dedicated to all kinds of mysteries." Posted on November 1, 2017, there was a two-paragraph write-up labeled **Murder of Rene Freer**. Whoever posted this spelled her first name wrong, which felt like another slight on the poor girl's memory. Here were the highlights from both paragraphs:

-Renee planned on playing with a friend up the street

-She was reported missing around 9:15

-Around 10:12, two firefighters found her body about 300 feet away from her home

-In 1999, the DNA was analyzed

The article's sources were a website called *Find a Grave* (morbid, for sure), an article from *The Hartford Courant* (oops, page not found!), and the aforementioned Savagewatch. Okay, I needed to find that article from the Hartford Courant. But I pressed on, skipped the Reddit threads that tried to connect a New Canaan resident named John Rice Jr. to the murder of Renee, and reviewed a site called *News and Clues*, which offered up its version of the "latest news, clues, offbeat, world events." A post that tagged Renee Freer was added on May 19, 2016. The title of the post was called **The Boogeyman**. Yet again, the name John Rice Jr. came up. He was the star of the piece because he killed a girl named Mary Mount with a rock. With conviction, the post's author relied on Savagewatch to declare facts of what happened to Renee. "Once again, the Boogeyman attacked and killed her."

I fully understood the need for any Boogeyman to exist in the brains of people who cared about Renee Freer's murder. It was much easier to grapple with. A Michael Myers-like force of nature invades a community, kills innocent kids, and then vanishes into the darkness. It's much harder to consider that a friend or family member could have killed Renee. But that's the angle I wanted to investigate before I joined the "John Rice Jr. did it" camp.

Finally, I reached the one article from The Bridgeport Post that seemed to carry more weight and credibility than anything else I could access. Written on June 24, 1977, the headline was POLICE QUIZ 'SEVERAL' IN MONROE GIRL'S SLAYING. A picture of a State Trooper and his bloodhound, Missy, was to the right of the text. I read the article once and kept going through it, comparing it to the other information I already had. New information to me:

-The cops questioned *many* adults and young people.

-Renee Freer was taken to St. Vincent's Medical Center. Sexual molestation was ruled out.

-The FBI was called in to test items while Nassau County was contacted to get fingerprints from the victim.

-Up to 28 regulars worked on the case.

-Someone contacted Lt. Gene Ready of New Canaan to see if there were any connections between the death of Mary Mount and that of Renee Freer. The John Rice Jr. angle couldn't be avoided as much as I tried.

While this information clearly communicated that the Monroe Police Department was committed to getting justice for Renee, I couldn't help but notice the inaccuracies from other sources to this one. Here, Renee's body was found by two *police* officers, while a different source said it was two *firefighters*. Additionally, this article claimed she was found 300 yards from her home (which equals three football fields), while two other sources said 300 feet. I needed to clear up some of these conflicting viewpoints, or else I would turn my mind off and tuck myself into bed at night with the possibility that John Rice Jr., a professional Boogeyman, was the guilty party after all.

THE SEARCH

I thought about the Wednesday night Renee was murdered.

On the eve of the last day of school.

The neighbors.

The parents.

Which ones helped?

Which ones didn't?

Had any of them pretended to help, knowing full well what had already happened to Renee? Had some sat inside rather comfortably, thinking that it was no big deal Renee was missing? Had someone known which man or boy committed this heinous act?

Could a girl have been involved?

Did the killer's parents learn of this and cover it up?

I had question after question after question.

And the only way to help Renee's cause was to address every one head-on.

AN OLD SAYING

After making an impromptu trip to Connecticut, I took a breather at Last Drop Coffee Shop and made small talk with a few old timers who had little interest in my book or the case. They seemed more interested in criticizing the local police force. As the conversation concluded, all but one of the men walked away. He reached over with his calloused hand and grabbed my shoulder. A smirk formed as he revealed, "There's an old saying in this town, Erik."

"Oh yeah? What's that?"

He snickered before continuing. "If anything happens in Monroe, the police department is usually the last place to hear about it."

The remark amused me. But a career in education taught me that there were good and bad apples and something else in between. I knew in my heart that Ken Heim was a good cop. I knew there were plenty of others, too. I just needed to move forward for the sake of Renee Freer and ignore what any of the townsfolk thought of the cops.

THE MONROE SUN

After leaving a few messages at the police department (the chief included), I checked my email and found a response from Bill Bittar, the head honcho at The Monroe Sun. This was my first response from a newspaper in Connecticut:

This is an interesting project. Renee was on my school bus. I was younger and remember my older sister introducing us during one ride. Her murder was the talk of the neighborhood, and I wrote about it as a reporter a couple times over the years.

I'd definitely be interested in talking to you about it when you're ready.

I was excited. Too excited. A legit reporter wanted to do a piece about Renee Freer (I stressed not to make it so much about me). I only wanted people to talk about her case.

Maybe Bill's efforts for The Monroe Sun could be the start of something positive. Just maybe.

JUST A DUDE WHO WATCHES DATELINE

While I waited for my students to arrive, I consumed an orange creamsicle kombucha and wondered when Chief White would call me back. Would my former stepfather call and tell me to stop pursuing this?

I wasn't alive when Renee Freer was murdered. I wasn't a cop. I wasn't a reporter or investigative journalist. I was just a dude who watched *Dateline* and *See No Evil* regularly and who got accepted into a Criminal Justice program. What did that even make me? Was I naïve for assuming that I could make a difference? Had I entered the Sean Penn phase of my life where I thrust myself into questionable situations? Would I have pursued justice for Renee if my former stepfather's name weren't listed as the point of contact for this case?

Embarrassingly, I don't think I would have.

Was I experiencing delusions of grandeur or just delusions? It all felt too coincidental, though. The one case from my town that intrigued me was the one that caused me to communicate with my former stepfather again. With all due respect for Ken, but I wouldn't have reached out to him for any other reason. If I heard about his passing and were available, I would try to go to his funeral. But I had no reason, after thirty-plus years of silence, to make contact. None whatsoever.

Except for the murder of Renee Freer.

Was her energy calling out to us?

Had she brought us back together, knowing it was the path to closure?

ALL POINTS TO RENEE

I couldn't process how Mrs. Freer felt. The fact that Renee's mother, Felicia, passed away before getting closure is another aspect that made me cling to this case.

If rumors swirled around town as suggested, how did the townsfolk allow this person to exist without paying for their crime? How did no one beat the living shit out of one of the persons of interest in an attempt to get a confession? I understood the importance of letting the detectives do their jobs, but the citizens also had to play a part.

Would a prosecutor say it all adds up to nothing but hearsay and circumstantial evidence? Perhaps. But someone knew something. Someone who didn't kill Renee goes to bed at night and lives with the truth stored in one of the crevasses in their brains. Were they still afraid to speak? Were they wondering if their information would do any good? Were they not enticed by the $50,000 reward? Was their privacy more important to them than securing justice for a long-dead girl?

Bill Bittar of The Monroe Sun wrote back and told me he wanted to do a story where I shared my most interesting findings.

My findings?

I had none.

I wanted to see the articles he wrote about her. I wanted to chat with him about meeting her on the bus. I wanted to chat with him about how the students and teachers acted post-murder.

But *I* had to deliver my findings?

I had to get the citizens of Monroe going somehow. I had to stoke a flame so it would catch fire throughout the entire community. As someone who loved avoiding people, I knew that I had to step out of my comfort zone and start being nice.

SCRAMBLING

I had no idea what I was doing.

Who the hell was I to try and get something going? I was a colossal nobody.

I thought about making flyers and stuffing them in the mailboxes of every Monroe resident, but I didn't live in the town or state anymore, and I didn't have the time or extra funds to commit to such an effort. I considered starting a Facebook group but dismissed it quickly because I didn't have many followers on my primary account.

At the start of COVID, I told my brother that I was sick of writing plays and wanted to try my hand at fiction. The notion always scared me because it was the type of writing I always started, stopped, and then quit. He ordered me to do one thing every day related to that cause. And while it didn't lead to notoriety, which I don't care about, it did lead to some publications with presses in the indie horror community. Why bring this up? Well, I thought of applying the same logic. Do one thing related to the Renee Freer case daily, and it will add up to something.

It would have to.

Because the Monroe Police was applying the same approach, right?

LIEUTENANT SOMETHINGOROTHER

Lt. Mac-something left me a voicemail. I was officially excited. What would he tell me? Would he ask for my email address and then send me scanned images of all the police reports?

Of course he would.

This is how naive I was.

I called him back; it went to voicemail. He returned my call shortly after that.

This Mc-somebody was pleasant to me. I turned off my inner Snape and was nice to him. And while I got the vibe that, in an alternate universe, he wanted to be helpful, he shared that he couldn't provide me with anything whatsoever because, get this, the case was active.

Forty-seven years of nothing, and yet it was still active.

I reminded him about the length of time since Renee's brutal murder. This wasn't just cold. It was ice cold. If this thing were any colder, it would be in Antarctica. His nice tone shifted, and he stated that cases weren't cold. They were active or closed.

If the cops couldn't help me and all I had was access to a few online articles, I had to do something bigger and more connected to the times.

I had to rely on using something I hadn't ever mastered: social goddamn media.

THE COLD CASE SITE

I visited CT.GOV-Connecticut's Official State Website and scrolled through the list of open cold cases.

Renee Freer wasn't listed on there.

But what the hell was the difference between an active case and an "open" cold case?

I trusted that Lt. Mc-Whatever was telling me the truth. But I pretended that I never had a chat with him and sent the following email to the Division of Criminal Justice:

Dear Cold Case Team,

Why isn't the Renee Freer case (Monroe, CT) from 1977 posted on your site? The case is still active and very unsolved.

Kindly,

Erik H

FACEBOOK WARNING

A friend in the horror community with ties to the reporting world warned me about creating a Facebook page devoted to Renee Freer's case. "It'll bring out all the crazies."

I heeded his advice but proceeded anyway.

I was a little crazy. My father was officially crazy. If the crazy was about to come, so be it.

What if it was a giant failure, though?

What if no one joined the group?

What would even happen if Renee's case were solved? The man or woman gets locked up, and the cops would throw a party. Then, people move on to their trivial or massive problems the next day.

Was it even worth the effort?

Then, I closed my eyes and thought of Renee Freer. Staring back at her killer. As they bashed her skull in.

I thought of Renee's mother dying in 2020 without getting closure.

I thought of my former stepfather visiting Renee's grave annually.

I thought of the killer living their life without ever getting caught.
And that's when I knew I had to keep going.
For as long as it took.

OBITUARY LEAD

One thing daily. Just one thing. I kept that mantra in my head as I searched for Felicia Freer's obituary. After finding it, I paused once I noticed the omission of Renee's name.

I understood and respected the decision. If my child were murdered when I was only 29 years of age, I wouldn't be able to handle it. If my child were murdered at any point in my life, it would be the same feeling.

Felicia's services and burial were private. There were no calling hours.

I found that to be tragic. Then again, COVID might have prevented the possibility of visitors.

In the left corner of the screen, there was a picture of three butterflies. I had no idea if the funeral home staff created this or if Felicia's son chose it. Regardless, I thought it represented mother, daughter (Renee), and son.

Moments later, I honed in on the name of Renee's brother and tried to locate where he lived. Once I confirmed his whereabouts, I decided to send a note to his workplace. It was a reach, but I didn't want to cold call him at home about his sister's unsolved murder. A simple and direct note via email felt like less of a bomb. I drafted the following message:

There is no easy way to start this message, so forgive me for reaching out to your place of business. But I am the author of ten books. I grew up in Monroe and wanted to write a piece about Renee Freer because I think it is beyond absurd that the case hasn't been solved after 47 years. Would you be willing to chat or trade emails? If so, we can try to put pressure on the powers that be to make this case feel less cold. I swear my intentions are good. If I don't hear from you, I totally understand. But I am prepared to shake as many trees as possible to get a person or two to come forward.

I sent the message and wished I could have crawled into my laptop and pulled the message back.

I felt sick inside. After the horrors he experienced, would you want to receive an email at your workplace from some dickhead writer? Would you want anyone reaching out about it?

No way.

If he replied and ordered me not to write a book about his slain sister, I would back away without protest and focus on the UMass Lowell program. I would go back to writing horror and Western books that a select few cared about.

COD AND ZUCCHINI

I buzzed my former stepfather around 8 p.m. one night. The TV was blasting in the background, so I had to wait to speak with him. Once we could hear each other, I told him I only needed five minutes of his time due to a forthcoming dinner of cod and zucchini.

I informed Ken that a Monroe detective called me back. He was shocked. It was as if he had a "spidey sense" and knew I would grill him about Renee Freer, so he switched gears to discuss my mother's health, his sister's dementia, and how often he saw his two daughters (my former stepsisters).

I wrangled this catch-up portion of the chat away from him and shared that two reporters (one from The Monroe Sun and another from CT Examiner) were interested in writing about Renee's case. Before I could even ask, he said he would be willing to chat with them.

Chat with the reporters, but not *me*?

I tried again to get him to spill the beans and give me the suspects' names. He said there weren't suspects, only persons of interest. I pressed him to tell me who the persons of interest were. He laughed as he rejected me again.

I found it admirable that this man, in his mid-70s, still upheld his integrity regarding the case. It was as if he felt he owed the department something even though he was completely out of touch with the current detective team. Part of me wanted to ask, "How much trouble could you really get into for giving me all the names of those interviewed?" But I didn't ask that question because I respected and cared about Ken too much.

NO REPLIES

No reply from multiple reporters at the CT Post.

Really?

Wasn't the case interesting enough?

Wasn't it heartbreaking enough?

I forgot about the reporters' lack of interest and thought about the Town Selectman of Monroe. My close friend Rick would later scream at me and insist that he was "the mayor and not the fucking Town Selectman!"

After eating nuts and veggie crisps (my feeble attempt to quit bread and eliminate my growing love handles), I tried to send a note to the Town Selectman's administrative assistant, but it kept asking me whether I wanted to use AOL, Google, or another application, so I decided to wait to send my note until later that evening.

While students worked in my room, I pulled up Google Earth to refresh my memory of Williams Drive.

Google Earth wouldn't load. I was ready to rage out like The Hulk. I was wearing a mask because one of the nameless students in my room was a chronic cougher/sneezer/sniffler who was, much to my chagrin, anti-tissues.

Google Earth finally opened! I punched in the address, but quickly recalled that it was renamed to Williams Road. After making that adjustment, I zoomed in and out on various sections via the Street View function. Even though it wasn't a road I ever frequented, I knew where it was located. It was right off Hattertown Road, a street not too far from where my friend Rick grew up.

Next, I punched in the address of my former stepfather's cabin. The wishbone driveway triggered me so much that I overlooked the decorative bunnies sitting outside a few days after the Easter holiday. Snippets of memories invaded my brain: the gun case on the balcony, the screened-in porch with ghastly green carpeting, the Playboy mags in the basement bathroom, the Steak-umms in the freezer, the labeled foods near the workbench, the stupid skylights (my mother's orders), the burnt orange fridge, Ken teaching me how to increase the heat of my fastball by extending my front leg more, *Dirty Dancing* playing on a loop while my stepsisters drove me insane, the kitchen stools on the floor so my youngest stepsister could hop over them and practice her horse riding skills sans horse, the Warrens visiting to see if a demon resided in the house, and, lastly, the gun going off and my friend—

I snapped out of this memory invasion and wondered what happened to my good friend. I was friends with two Greg Fs growing up, but I wasn't friends with either one now. Did that say something about time passing or more about the kind of person I became?

UNFORGIVABLE TYPO

Instead of waiting for the leading reporters from the CT Post to give a damn about Renee Freer's case, I flipped through various online articles, hoping to find a reporter that seemed fairly new to the field. I reached out to Kayla Mutchler. Moments after pitching the case to her via email, I wanted to die. There was a typo in my subject line. I had written this: *Author hopes to she light on unsolved murder case in Monroe.*

<u>She</u> light?!

I interned at The New Group while I attended NYU from 2011-2013. Prominent playwrights would submit a cover letter, along with their latest manuscript. If there were a typo in the letter, the literary manager would discard everything. Regardless of their standing in the field.

I couldn't get over my typo.

There was no way in the world that Kayla would reply.

She shouldn't. She couldn't.

But she did just that only two and a half hours after I sent her the message. She revealed that she was going to write a piece about Renee's case!

I felt good with a CT Post article lined up and the one that Bill Bittar was going to write for The Monroe Sun. Even though I was a typo-writing jackass.

ATTENTION

A few people I cared about accused me of doing this for attention.

The book.

The Facebook group.

And I wholeheartedly understood how anyone could perceive it that way. But my immediate counter would be as follows: Doesn't a 47-year-old murder mystery deserve more attention than a few articles online? Shouldn't there be an annual reminder that the cops never solved Renee Freer's case? Why did my interest in criminal justice and true crime have to be framed in a manner of selfishness?

People's lack of interest for a case they had knowledge of was selfish to me.

I knew what my intentions were. My former stepfather connected me to this case—end of story. I wasn't going to waste time explaining my reasoning any further.

Renee Freer's case needed a jolt of exposure, and I knew how to provide it.

Was I in love with reporters wanting to frame articles around my writing? No. But it would be a new article and conversation for the citizens of Monroe and the state of Connecticut to have. What was the harm in that?

My brother was quick to remind me of potential dangers with a DM on Instagram. "Murderers don't like to be chased."

Yeah, yeah, yeah.

But fuck the people that participated in Renee's murder.

Was it one, two, or ten?

The number didn't matter.

Fuck them all.

SLIPPERY FISH

People reached out to me on Facebook, wanting to discuss Renee Freer's murder.

Some shared their wild theories, while others provided helpful information. I reminded them to call or email the police.

That's when some went quiet. That's when some left the group.

I couldn't understand the dichotomy between wanting justice and remaining silent. What was I going to do with helpful information? Add it to my book? Who cared about adding a juicy story if it never landed on the cops' desks? I grew tired of listening to armchair detectives that wanted to go on ad nauseam yet didn't want to do anything about it.

I didn't know how the cops did it.

There was a delicacy that I needed to understand.

Plus, a mammoth amount of time had passed.

Was the community still in denial?

Was the community still healing?

Does this type of murder take that long to recover from?

Was it reasonable to assume that many had forgotten most of the details of what occurred to Renee?

WANT TO DE-STRESS?

I cruised through the hallways of my school, mentally dreaming up all the ways I could generate more attention for Renee Freer's case. I stopped in front of a paper sign on the wall. It asked, "*Want to de-stress?*"

I nodded as if I were speaking with a person and then looked down at the tan desk. There was a printout that provided two strategies to eliminate stress: deep belly breathing and bumblebee breathing. The directions for the former were too difficult for my brain to process, so I returned to my room and focused on the directions for the second option.

1. sit

2. rub your hands

3. reach arms up as you breathe

4. breathe out, lower arms to side

5. hum a buzz sound

While the exercise calmed me, my brain merged toward a negative place. Why was I doing this?

My little book wouldn't solve the murder.

My little book would come and go, and then the lights would go out on Renee Freer again.

The energy of the Facebook group would eventually peter out, too.

There would never be justice for Renee Freer.

Breathe out, hum a buzz. Repeat.

I realized that there was no room, not even a single inch, for apathy on this quest.

It wasn't my job to solve a thing, though. That was the responsibility of the Monroe Police. My future book and the Facebook group were exposure tools. Nothing more, nothing less. Once I accepted that reality, everything came into focus.

EVERYWHERE A RUMOUR

This was the "I heard" case.

One of my former classmates at Masuk heard that a foster kid did it.

A friend of a retired cop heard that they had their man but could never secure the confession.

One middle-aged woman messaged me point blank on Facebook and said a brother and sister duo were responsible.

One woman swore that a cop murdered Renee and spent his life covering it up.

A pair of friends insisted that it was one of two people with the same first name.

I heard that a girl walked into school the day after the murder, announced that Renee Freer was dead, and then judged her peers for getting emotional about it.

I heard that the killer, due to his prolonged grief, committed suicide many years ago.

I heard Renee wasn't raped, yet there was a bite mark on her body.

I heard a teddy bear contaminated the bite mark.

I heard there was an apple near her dead body.

I heard the cops exhumed Renee's body a few days after her burial.

I heard the cops never exhumed Renee's body.

I also heard that the cops exhumed Renee's body in 1999.

A pair of brothers heard that a teen with a short temper and a fondness for wife-beater tanks killed Renee.

A distant relative of the victim heard that two young men visited Renee's grave in Stratford for days after her burial.

I heard a well-known psychic got a bad vibe from one of the younger cops and refused to help the force out any further.

A Facebook user commented that there was a teen in the area who killed cats on a regular basis. Therefore, he must have graduated to offing young girls.

A person who frequented Hattertown Road and Williams Drive thought it was a mentally challenged boy. As if the mere existence of such a person meant he/she should be suspect number one.

A business owner heard that the cops questioned one family aggressively, which caused said family to move out of town immediately. Another business owner agreed with everything but the *immediately* part. He said the guilty party moved in the winter of 1978.

I heard new houses were being built and that a white van was seen lingering in the neighborhood that dreadful evening.

Others reached out, revealing that they had "a feeling" about what had occurred since they knew someone who dated a person of interest.

Many people found the articles about John Rice Jr. and announced that it was CASE CLOSED!

One man frequently asked why Renee's mother went to the grocery store (as if this wasn't common for a parent) and how she could have left her daughter alone with her grandparents.

I appreciated the rumors since they made my ears perk up each time, but I had to sift through the information that lacked objectivity. The only questions that simmered on my mind were these: Who lived in Renee Freer's neighborhood, and who did she play with regularly? I could branch out and see how far the web went by starting there.

EX-STEPSISTER #2

I received a message from my other ex-stepsister. The younger one. The one that used to put goddamn stools on the floor and hop over them like she was training for her next horse show. God, I missed her. Or that version of her. I had no idea what kind of adult she became. Her message read:

It was so awesome to have you reach out to my dad! I have thought about you so often throughout the years. You and I got along so well! (Well, at least that is how I remember it). You seem to be doing so great! I had no idea you were an author. I'm very interested in reading your books.

I am sure it was quite a trip speaking to my dad. He's had a rough life. But he has always meant well!

How is your mom? I always loved your mom. She was always so kind to us.

Not one to be emotional, this message landed. I couldn't explain why. To say that about my mother? Or was it to hear that someone thought about me over the years? It was nice to hear that. Even though this stepsister drove me crazy 24/7, I would concede during a polygraph that I sometimes missed her too.

I hadn't even met with Ken yet. Would I get the chance to do so before he passed? Would I ever see my ex-stepsisters again?

Part of me hoped so. But all of my energy was focused on helping the world of Connecticut learn about what happened to Renee Freer and convince a few of them to help get justice for her.

THE MONROE SUN

(April 14, 2024)

A new article from The Monroe Sun went live, and I learned that the Monroe Police Department worked with Quantico on the Freer case because they had the latest tools.

So, the cops had something valuable in terms of DNA. They had to, right?

I shoved my thoughts aside and kept reading. Norman Mercier, a retired detective who worked the case, offered his thoughts: "It was a violent murder, and a child was involved. Whenever you have a child involved it makes matters 10 times worse. It was something that never happened in the town of Monroe before — and it's never happened since, so it was a shock to the whole community." I processed the quote, knowing full well it must have shocked everyone. But what went wrong? I wondered what altered Renee's fate and led to her never getting justice.

In the article, Keith White, the Chief of Police, revealed that there were three murders in the state that day. Since the Chief Medical

Examiner's office was short-staffed, a decision was made: one of the first detectives on scene had Renee Freer's battered body sent to St. Vincent's, where she received a hospital autopsy.

If she had a forensic autopsy, White implied that more evidence would have been preserved and could have been examined years later due to the advancements in technology.

He said all murder victims now receive forensic autopsies.

Now?

Wasn't that great news for Renee Freer and her surviving family members?

WTF

Why and the hell didn't the cops wait for Renee Freer to get a forensic autopsy?

All murders were tragic, yes. But if three occurred in Connecticut that day, why didn't the eight-year-old girl with the Hollywood smile get first priority?

HOSPITAL AUTOPSY VS. A FORENSIC ONE

I contacted OCME (the Office of the Chief Medical Examiner) in Connecticut and spoke with a woman. I told her I needed immediate clarification on the differences between a hospital autopsy and a forensics one. She said she would email me an answer later in the day. She honored her word and sent me the following response:

Good afternoon,

I have found an answer for you.

There is no difference in technique for a hospital vs. a forensic autopsy. The main difference is who does them. Forensic autopsies are done by board-certified forensic pathologists, while most hospital autopsies are performed by hospital pathologists. Most hospital pathologists are not board-certified forensic pathologists, which requires an additional fellowship year of training.

Hope this helps!

It didn't!

It was stupid. This woman wasn't stupid. But this token response from OCME was.

Annoyed beyond measure, I reached out to Norman Mercier, the retired detective who was in charge of the Renee Freer investigation. Fortunately, he clarified more: "To me, it's like night and day. Like a plumber versus an electrician. I mean, one is trained to check out for cancers, where the other one is just trying to find out the cause of death."

Why hadn't the cops waited with Renee's body in the woods until she could get the proper autopsy? Why had they handed over power to a hospital that wasn't professionally equipped to handle it?

Had they not done so, Renee Freer might have gotten justice years ago.

IMPORTANCE OF THE CRIME SCENE

I flipped through the book written by Paul Holes, strictly thinking about the first cops at Renee's murder scene. "Most investigators follow a standard routine and don't take the time to study what happened. They are off and running, tracking down witnesses and leads before they've ever assessed what happened and why." Holes continued, "A lot of times, crime scene investigators follow the detective's lead without questioning whether the evidence matches the theory (175)." I had to consider that times had significantly changed from 1977, and that Holes might be speaking about today's approach versus strategies from the past. But I couldn't argue with his one particular belief about doing everything in one's power to get justice. "One of the things I'd learned over the years was to never skip that extra step if your gut tells you to take it, even if it seems unlikely to produce anything of significance. You owe the victim that consideration (177)."

Someone didn't take that extra step for Renee. They rushed her off to the hospital, and in doing so, relinquished every bit of power they had.

THE VICTIM'S LOCATION AND DNA

A few newspaper articles suggested the cops found Renee 300 yards from her home. One article said 300 feet (100 yards). I fought with my brain to stress that this was in 1977 not 2024. There were no cell phones. Was all the confusion the result of such a traumatic murder for the small town of Monroe?

Forgiving an inaccuracy about the distance, I wondered what DNA the cops still had access to.

The failure to close the case for Renee Freer suggested that the DNA testing wasn't up to snuff or that the police had no valuable evidence. If that was the case, where was the fucking rock? Did the DNA wear off over time? Was it the type of object that wouldn't produce reliable fingerprints? I couldn't think about the rock or its current condition. Wherever it might be. But if this was a waiting game for the DNA world to advance, I knew my next move was contacting a new age company, generating tons of national attention for their efforts.

Moments later, I contacted Othram.

OTHRAM!

I couldn't believe I got a response from the place that employed Paul Holes. The place that was changing the game in how cases got solved.

Erik,

I appreciate you reaching out. We will see if there is something we can do to help.

Best,

David

Under the HOW YOU CAN HELP tab, it said that if DNA was uploaded, it could "help law enforcement better home in on a suspect, kind of like sonar for solving crimes."

I wondered what the cops had. Could they still test the blood on the rock? Was there an article of clothing on file to test? In conjunction with the efforts of Paul Holes, this company helped catch the Golden State Killer. If they wanted to help, this case would end. A suspect would emerge, and the cops would arrest them within the year. The days of hiding in plain sight were over, motherfucker. You're done, done, done.

Othram was going to help with the case!

THE MONROE SUN AGAIN

(APRIL 18, 2024)

The Monroe Sun ran another article, reminding readers that this was Monroe's only unsolved murder. Chief White said, "This incident has had a negative effect on many lives, including the suspect and his family who have lived with this for 47 years."

Has it had a negative effect on the killer's family, though? It seemed like they never wanted to pony up the goods for Renee Freer. It seemed like they could totally live with this.

White continued, "We believe a juvenile, known to Renee, committed this crime. We are appealing to the suspect or his family to come forward with even the smallest pieces of information. We are confident they know more than what has been disclosed in the past."

I knew how I would define the term juvenile, but I raced to Justice.gov to see how they referred to it in their criminal resource manual.

A "juvenile" is a person who has not attained his eighteenth birthday." I paused before continuing. The emphasis on the word *his* bothered me. Couldn't a girl be a juvenile, too? I read the rest: *"Juvenile delinquency" is the violation of a law of the United States committed by a person prior to his eighteen birthday which would have been a crime if committed by an adult.*

There was *his* again.

So, were the cops suggesting a male known to Renee did this or was the emphasis on *his* an archaic way to go about explaining terminology in the manual about criminals?

I read all of Chief White's words again. "We are appealing to the suspect or his family to come forward with even the smallest pieces of information."

His family? Right there. I missed it the first time. But here was the Chief revealing that it was a male.

I got out of my head and focused on the follow-up statement from Chief White: "This will bring the case to a conclusion for the sake of Renee, her remaining family and the community as a whole."

I appreciated Chief White's efforts on the matter. However, the quote assumed that the killer's family cared about Renee, her family, and the Monroe community. I didn't think they cared about anything but their freedom.

A freedom they didn't deserve.

CT POST

(APRIL 19, 2024)

Sonuvabitch.

I should be pissed off that the reporter named my city of residence and place of employment in the latest article about Renee Freer's case, but I was more unnerved by Monroe's Chief of Police walking back his statement from the previous day.

In this article, White clarified that "right now, there's not a specific person that's been identified."

Not a specific person?! What was this maneuver?

Was it a male juvenile close to Renee or not?

Why would the Chief of Police walk this back? No one was named. Why had he walked back a statement that had medium power and diluted the hell out of it?

If the killer caught this statement, he probably laughed his ass off. If the killer was, in fact, a male teen. This certainly opened the door back up to it being anybody, as in, any gender. If they didn't know who did it, they didn't have anything valuable. How could Othram help with that?

Perhaps I misinterpreted the Chief's words. Because if I hadn't, there was no telling who committed this crime. It was then and only then that I hoped the Boogeyman of Connecticut was responsible.

RENEE IS MISSING

Who was there first?

Firemen as the old papers suggest?

Or was it the cops?

Stephen Biley, a Monroe cop who lived at 16 Williams Drive at the time, confirmed that he was home for dinner but received the call about a missing girl while on duty. After making it to where Hattertown meets Route 59, he headed back to his neighborhood and became the first responder. As for the firemen arriving, Biley revealed, "That was me. I called them in. It was getting dark, so I called headquarters."

David Lizak, a 14-year-old junior firefighter at the time, revealed that the search for Renee started around 9:45 p.m. and that the fire department got there first in conjunction with the people who were already searching for Renee. "It was a warm evening and once she was found, everyone was flabbergasted. It's just been something that's stayed with me for years."

Carol Pekar Ogrinc, a resident from the neighborhood at the time, elaborated on how it felt to be thrust into the chaos of the night. "That same evening was Chalk Hill's 8th grade graduation. I was at the graduation that evening, and when I came home, my friends came to my house and told me Renee was missing, and they couldn't find her. My friends and I went up the street and saw many police and other volunteers looking for her. What has always stood out most about that night was her mother's reaction when she was told Renee was found. I think it was around 11 p.m. I could remember where she was standing when I heard her scream. There were people holding her back because she wanted to go to her daughter. That's just something that's etched in my mind and probably will be forever."

LORRAINE WARREN
(Yeah, the famous one)

"I slept in Renee's room."

Taken aback by Stephen Biley revealing this, I asked him why on earth he would do this and how the police force would allow it. "Lorraine Warren felt that since Renee was murdered, her spirit could be going around, and it's possible she could come back to her surroundings."

And when I asked if Renee came back, he chuckled: "There was a clock, a black cat, okay, with a white stomach. It was a kid's clock. It wasn't working. We had the whole night recorded. When we listened to the recording, the clock was ticking."

My family had their own experiences with the Warrens, so I wasn't surprised by such an event happening.

Had it brought the Monroe Police Department any closer to figuring out anything significant to the case? No, but it revealed an energy from the deceased beyond the grave. Renee was communicating back then, and as hokey as it must sound, she reconnected me with my former family and allowed one of my closest friends to reconnect with his.

Could her spirit want justice?

Hell yes.

DELIRIUM

I lost track of days and times due to my newfound obsession.

I kept reviewing the old articles about Renee's case while reporters generated new ones framed around me. Some articles got my name wrong. Some said my book had already been released. Some shared personal details, yet they weren't entirely accurate about my current work status or location.

While one would think I was elated by the exposure, I wanted this strictly centered around Renee.

But if I had to be the tip of the spear to get the attention going again, I would do so.

My friend Rick became as obsessed as I did, which only motivated me to keep coming up with ideas.

I pitched *Dateline*, *Unsolved Mysteries*, and *Cold Justice*. During that period of silence, I created a petition for Renee and called out Governor Lamont (and his predecessor) for not increasing the reward for helpful information.

A few days after doing so, I deleted the petition because, asshole that I was, I wasn't aware that the maximum reward was $50,000. Bill Bittar from The Monroe Sun played spoiler by sharing this law with me: "**Sec. 54-48. Reward for arrest of capital offender or felon.** When any crime punishable by death or imprisonment for more than one year has been committed, the Governor, upon application of the state's attorney for the judicial district in which it has been committed, may offer, publicly, a reward not exceeding fifty thousand dollars, to the person who gives information leading to the arrest and conviction of the guilty person, or, if such guilty person has fled after conviction of a felony in a court of this state, to the person who gives information leading to the arrest and detention of the convicted felon, whether found within the state or elsewhere, which reward shall be paid to the informer by the state, by order of the court before which such conviction is had."

Rookie move.

But as I stated earlier, I was not a detective or a reporter. I was just a dude who...

...was running out of ideas. But Rick kept my interest high with his "it's too late to quit" energy.

He wouldn't simply let me attempt a book and get away with it. He wanted more. Not for me or him but the town we grew up in. Yes, we once trashed Monroe as a place where there was nothing to goddamn do growing up, but our fondness for it grew once we left town and started our adult lives.

I missed the burgers and fries at Bill's Drive-In. The tennis courts at Wolfe Parke. The trails at Great Hollow. The sound of the bats hitting baseballs at Beardsley Field. Ice cream sandwiches from Carvel. Cheerleader Fridays at Masuk High School. Open rec basketball. Torturing our teacher in Spanish class. Mario Bernardi's daily antics.

This could have been us. It could have happened to our classmates.

The town secret needed to end, and we needed to do it for Renee Freer. To keep myself motivated, I contacted some of Renee's friends after they commented or posted in the group.

JUNE 23, 1977

(ONE DAY AFTER RENEE'S MURDER)

Kerri Keeler was one of Renee Freer's closest friends. She recalled the day following the murder; it was her last day of the year at Stepney Elementary. "I remember the layout of our classroom the day our class was told Renee was gone. You walked in and straight across from that door was our coatroom, to the left our class all seated at round tables. Mrs. Sampley's desk was on the left front corner as you stepped into the room. That's where she was, head down into her folded arms, audibly sobbing in a way I had never heard an adult audibly sob. Our table was in the back just beside the coatroom. Abby, Renee, and I sat together at that table. Every day. Just us three. But that day it was just me and Abby. Everything we'd known was about to get turned upside down on its head. And this was the last day of school. Welcome to summer. BAM."

Sandy Banks, a Reading Consultant, said, "I don't remember anyone referring to her death as a murder in the beginning. Teachers and staff were in shock as nothing like this had ever happened to anyone we knew before. There was a feeling of confusion as none of us knew how to react to the news. We didn't know how to prepare for questions that students would have."

The Stepney Elementary population was blindsided. The community of Monroe was changed forever. And the stain of Renee's murder wouldn't be wiped off until the killer was caught.

No pressure for the Monroe Police Department. None at all.

GIGGLES

Renee's nickname was Giggles.

Someone killed a girl nicknamed Giggles?

That was enough to wage war.

I stared at the posted picture of her third-grade class. No one stood out more than Renee.

She leaped off the photo, reaching out with that beaming smile and innocent eyes. If eyes were the window to the soul, Renee had more soul than most of us combined. Tawny Syrotiak, a member in the Facebook group, posted this: "She had the most infectious laugh. I can still hear her. Renee was one of my very first friends. I lived down the street from her. We shared the same school bus and had the same class. I think of her often and pray that this case is solved and brings closure to so many of us."

One of Renee's other friends from the time, Abby Mae Rowell, has never forgotten her. "We were best friends. I will never forget her. She slept over my house the weekend before she was murdered. We both slept outside in my brother's tree house. It was a big deal for us. We had a hundred-foot extension cord that ran through the yard. We were scared, ended up running back and forth to the house and the fort. We ended up sleeping inside! She wrote me a card and made me a drawing. It was a heart, which she had written friends forever! My mom framed it. I am fifty-six-years-old. It's been hanging on my wall for forty-five years.... still forever eight-years old. She was sweet and caring. Always smiling and happy girl. Taken too soon."

As I went forward with my research, I studied photos of people who "might" know something. I stared into their eyes. For some, I would ask, *"Do you know something? How about you? Have a little info you want to share?"* And by the law of averages, I stumbled upon a few pictures and studied the eyes for minutes on end. For a select few, I thought, *"You know what happened that June evening. Those eyes betray you. If you only knew how much those eyes lied."*

Laura Johnson wasn't as close to Renee as the others but felt compelled to weigh in on how the eight-year-old changed her life for the better. "Giggles was a friend when I really needed one. We lived exactly a mile apart. The bus picked her up after me. I was shy and awkward and sat alone on the bus. Everyone had their friends, buddied up. I would carry a book with me to pretend that it didn't matter. Giggles saw through that. She was so young and yet knew exactly what I needed – a friend. Giggles made it a point to sit by me and talk to me daily (and make me laugh, of course). She's the only one who did that. I loved her for that. It also kept others from making fun of me."

But once Renee was murdered, it changed everything for Laura. "After her murder, every day the bus drove past her stop, I couldn't help but cry. There has never been another Giggles in my life."

THE AFTERMATH

Perhaps more than wanting to know every detail about Renee's murder, I was equally curious about how the community reacted in the days that followed. Carol Pekar Ogrinc, nearly fourteen at the time, said, "After that night, the neighborhood didn't seem the same. We didn't want to go out and play and if we did, we stayed very close to the house. We became more vigilant and were suspicious of any cars we didn't recognize." Brian Laychak, who was one grade ahead of Renee and shared the bus with her, further supported Carol's beliefs. "Her murder affected everyone in our small community. Parents and kids alike. That event took all of our innocence and kindness away. I remember walking around with a baseball bat and walkie-talkie that summer and not allowed to go into the woods. We were all too afraid the murderer was still out there."

Cathi Tyszka Taylor, sixteen at the time of Renee's murder, shared her take: "Moms were afraid, dads were angry. It was a little crazy. Had there been social media and the like at the time, it would have been out of control. Certainly, Monroe was not immune to crime but murder?"

IN THE KILLER'S HEAD

After the killer ended Renee Freer's life, where did they go?

Home? With blood all over their clothes?

Or did they cut through the wooded paths that led to Knapp Street and go to a friend's house to produce an alibi?

Many townsfolk shared that there were graduation parties that evening.

Had the killer blended in at onc of those gatherings?

REJECTED FUNDS, POLICE LOGS

After Renee's murder, Stepney Elementary School tried to start a fund for her surviving family members, but they canceled it. Did Renee's parents want to pretend that it never happened? Or was heavy support from the community more detrimental than good to the emotions of the horrifying situation?

July 4th came and went. Cops eliminated suspects.

And what?

The killer settled back into normalcy twelve days later? They smoked pot, tossed back beers, and pretended they didn't kill Renee while all of their buddies wondered who was responsible?

I learned that the Monroe Police Department created a special phone number for Renee's case. Were so many calls coming in that they needed a new, separate line? Was there even a voicemail service, or was it a live line with an officer sitting at a desk?

I reviewed a newspaper clipping from July 17, 1977, with the headline MURDER TOPS POLICE LOG IN MONROE.

I would hope so.

Renee's name should be at the top of every log and police blotter ever since.

It reminded me how much everyone had forgotten her.

And that was inexcusable. If the cops have been turning over every stone throughout the years, what were reporters doing? Shrugging their shoulders and letting time pass? Was there no working reporter besides Bill Bittar and Kayla Mutchler that gave a current damn about Renee Freer? It certainly seemed that way.

I had a reporter lined up at the CT Examiner. He lost interest in doing an article about Renee. Translation: He didn't care about her. If he had, he would have whipped something up for her cause.

There was no room for competition here. People had to do their part. The alternative was unacceptable.

SELF-PRESERVATION

Is that all this was?

A teen that knew Renee killed her because they wanted to see what it felt like?

Or had a game gotten out of hand?

Had they stared at Renee's smashed face, someone they labeled a friend, and grasped the magnitude of what they had done?

Had they recruited friends or siblings to cover for them?

Or was this the clever work of shocked parents?

What a sick joke.

The joke wasn't on the killer, though; it was on everyone else. Renee's family. The cops. The town of Monroe. Meanwhile, they cruised through the community, pretending not to know about the murder.

The years ticked by, and they had kids. They learned how wrong it was to kill because they surely wouldn't want anyone killing any of their kids. And there's the irony.

Self-preservation. It's inside every single one of us.

But fuck this guy.

Or woman.

They should know better.

The only answer is that they still don't give a single shit about Renee. I would argue that they never did. Regardless of the tricks they pulled to try and suggest otherwise.

WE ALL HAVE OUR SECRETS

Aside from my biological father's run-ins with the law and my first stepfather working the Freer case unbeknownst to me while I lived in his cabin for a few years, I had one of my own secrets.

Greg F was the smartest and most fearless kid I knew growing up. His moppy hair and thicker frame betrayed how smart and devious he was. At that age, the devious was a good thing. Whenever I arrived at his home, I was always surprised by what the day entailed. One day, he came out the front door with a new bow and arrow. Another day, he had multiple Chinese stars in his possession.

Beyond his affinity for weapons, he was the catcher on my baseball team. For a short clip in my life, I was a dominant pitcher who threw a mean fastball. Every catcher but him would lean back or shiver once I cranked my arm back and let it fly.

Not Greg. Never Greg.

He would sit in a crouched position, almost bored by the speed of my pitches as the batters, more times than not, missed making contact with the ball.

I knew where his fearlessness came from. But I always wondered if there was something that could scare him.

One evening at my former stepfather's cabin, Greg and I played in the furnished basement. To my recollection, the game was some form of Cowboys and Indians (Yes, I know. Not a game one should play anymore). Getting lost in the game of pretend, the game of good guy versus bad guy, I ventured into the room connected to the garage. There was a huge shelf to the left with labeled boxes and containers of food (my first stepfather was territorial about his favorite snacks). Off to the right was a lengthy workbench with every tool known to man. As I backed up to escape my pretend enemy, Greg pretended to toss something my way. Despite the laughter that took over the moment, we both shared a competitive energy to defeat one another, so I grabbed a pistol at the end of the workbench, aimed it, and fired it at his face.

The pistol had never gone off before.

But here it had.

The sound rang out, causing me to drop the pistol and hold my ears. I stared at Greg, whose eyes were as big as saucers. I expected him to fall to his knees and keel over. I feared I would have to run upstairs and get my stepfather, lying on the floor in a robe, watching a classic action film.

But Greg didn't move a muscle.

Shortly after the shock of him not being shot and no one upstairs hearing this, we stood across from one another.

Game over. Friendship over?

I hoped not.

But in time, I knew it was over.

Greg returned to the basement area and went into the green-colored bathroom. He stared at himself in the mirror. Before I knew what he was doing, he opened his mouth wide. This was the place where we would snag the Playboy mags.

Then I saw it.

White tongue.

Official proof Greg could get scared.

Minutes later, we walked upstairs, passed my stepfather as we said, "Goodnight," and went up a second stairwell to my stepsisters' vacant bedroom. Greg got into his bed; I got into mine.

We exchanged a few words and went to sleep.

And it's now I wondered: What would I have done had I blown his face off? Would I have called out to my stepfather or mother for immediate assistance? Or would I have dragged his body outside, tossed his dead ass in the woods, and hoped to create an elaborate lie that would shift all the blame off of me?

The truth is, I have no clue. But is this what happened in the woods behind Williams Drive? Had a game of doctor gotten out of hand? Had they been playing their version of Cowboys and Indians, and Renee became an accidental casualty?

Possibly.

But I remembered that she was hit with the rock more than once.

No accident.

Ripped shirt.

Had someone tried to rape her, or had someone simply grabbed her because she was trying to get away from what was about to happen to her?

I tuned out the idea that Renee knew she was going to be murdered because the thought was too much to bear.

Because of my unforgettable experience with Greg, I completely understood how a lie could be created and carried. But for forty-seven years?!

Who could hold onto that for a friend? Or a sibling?

Had I killed my best friend growing up, I don't think I could have held onto that secret for forty-seven minutes.

But we all have secrets on our life résumés, ranging from minor ones to evil acts.

SHOPPING

I follow Felicia Freer through Monroe Supermarket.

The dark and dank interior doesn't do any favor for marketing the products on the shelves.

Felicia Freer cruises through the first aisle. I trail behind her, reminding her she is here to buy baked goods and nothing more.

"Chop, chop," I say.

But she moseys through the long aisles, enjoying the momentary freedom from watching her children yet knowing they are in good hands with her parents.

"Make it snappy. You have to get back home."

I get ticked off at her for not listening, but I realize, even during this daydream, that she can't hear me.

Why am I a ghostlike visitor?

She makes it to the Baking Needs section, and I glance at the massive clock on the back wall.

I sense that Renee is in trouble, so I scream at the top of my lungs. "Forget making treats for school tomorrow. Get home now before it's too late!"

She picks up a bag of chocolate chips.

The clock ticks.

She studies the bag and puts it back on the shelf.

The clock ticks.

She picks up two different boxes of brown sugar.

The indecision tortures me.

I glance at the register station and see that there are only two cashiers available. Both move slowly and have long lines of customers.

I reach for Felicia's hand and attempt to grab it.

But nothing happens.

She grabs a small bottle of vanilla extract.

The clock ticks.

And ticks.

And ticks.

And ticks.

I collapse onto the floor in the middle of the dirty aisle.

I know the event of Renee's murder is in motion, and at this point, there is nothing that her mother, or anyone else, can do about it.

HANNIBAL

Like most people, my wife had the hots for Mads Mikkelsen.

Amusement aside, I recalled an episode from the show *Hannibal* where he delivered a line that bounced around my brain for days after I heard it.

"There's no morality. Only morale."

Was that all the killer had to do? Control morale for 47 years? Convince their family members that everything would be okay if morale remained positive?

SPECIAL PLACE IN HELL

Flames surround me.

Nothing but goddamn flames.

Am I in a cave?

No, no.

I am moving down, which means I am in some sort of elevator.

I hate the heat, so this is rather uncomfortable for me.

I close my eyes, stick out my tongue (as if that would help), and wait until I hit the bottom floor.

The elevator slams against the ground, and the doors open. A yellow sign greets me. It says, SPECIAL PLACE IN HELL.

Having no more enemies to speak of (or so I think), I wonder what I am doing here, and then I see them.

There is a small group of three. Flames surround them, but they are all intact. They look like a woman and two men. I walk closer to confirm my suspicions. They don't seem worried about my presence because their eyes are glued to a small Zenith TV. It looks like a model from the 1970s.

I wipe my brow because the heat is unbearable, but I endure it because I want to see what this trio is watching.

I bend down and see the woods.

The homes.

And then I see the kids. This trio of pre-teens and teens and then little Renee—innocent and obliviously hanging out with the older group.

The crime unfolds before my eyes, and I can't look. I turn around and realize that the devil is behind me.

I ask, "You make them watch this shit?"

"On repeat," the Devil says.

"Why?"

"Until one of them confesses to Renee's murder."

"Have any of them done that yet?"

"Still waiting. But I'll beat anyone in the game of patience."

ONE OF TWO GREGS

I tried to reach the Greg I almost murdered many moons ago. Getting his take on the evening I nearly blew his head off was essential. To see how he remembered versus how I did. But after contacting his family and doing an extensive search, I couldn't find him.

He was more challenging to find than the persons of interest in the Renee Freer case.

I repeat: He was more challenging to find than the persons of interest in the Renee Freer case.

I'll let you all process that.

VIDEO FOOTAGE?

Before my workday started, I called Rick. We made idiotic sounds (mature for men in their mid-40s) and reminisced about how we tortured Mrs. Young in Spanish class. We yucked it up about who we had crushes on and who we disliked immensely.

Rick bragged about bombing out on quizzes early in a marking period and then calculating the exact score he needed to achieve a 70 average.

But then we talked about the Freer case. We wondered who the cops interviewed and what those transcripts looked like. I told him it could be hard to detect tone from how the reports were written.

And then Rick said, "There was no video back then, either."

I felt so stupid.

But was he right? I wasn't sure. If he was right, a detective had to study a piece of paper and decide who was worth bringing back for an interview and who wasn't without the ability to study speech patterns and body language.

It was more important than ever to get people to go to the police. Not just for their helpful information but so they could be recorded on camera.

JUVENILE VS. ADULT – OMFG

A person close to me remarked, "I am pretty shocked that the killer hasn't turned himself in yet." Amused, I asked why. "Well, he did this as a juvenile, which means he couldn't be tried as an adult."

I was so dumb. I never considered this.

DO YOU HAVE TO GO BACK TO THE TIME OF WHAT THE LAW WAS?

YES.

I hated the justice system. My father was sentenced to 40 years and only served 9. A teen could kill a young girl and do zero time for it because they aged out of the crime.

It was so unfair.

It was more salt on the 47-year-old wound.

RENEE ACTUALLY STRUGGLED

It was confirmed.

Renee struggled with her killer.

Whatever was found under the fingernails proved as much.

The killer yanked her halter top down.

Was this a failed attempt at rape? She fought back, and her killer retaliated? A "how dare you" for resisting?

I wanted to believe that this was an accident. Messing about in the woods went way too far before the killer realized it was much too late to do anything but try to cover up what he or she had done.

But this was worse.

This was cruel. How cruel? Stephen Biley, working patrol for the Monroe Police at the time, highlighted the manner in which Renee was killed with the rock. "He put her head several inches into the ground."

This was beyond cruel; it was plain evil.

The question remained: Was this really the sadistic work of a male teen, or was it a male adult? Or was it the work of both?

THE CHILD STAR

A group member posted an article from The Hartford Courant that I had never seen before.

At first, I couldn't make heads or tails of it, so I read it a few more times.

The piece's author interviewed kids, which seemed wrong for multiple reasons. While a nameless boy provided a quote for the article, a girl's name was listed for all to read. She was one of Renee's best friends and the unquestioned star of the article. Her first quote? "All the kids are inside." Okay, that one made sense. Her second quote? "My mother won't let me go to the bus stop alone." There was only one day of school left. Who would care about this? Who would refer to this type of inconvenience instead of revealing how traumatized they were?

The article was posted two days after the murder, so the reporter interviewed these two kids one day after the murder.

I had to stop judging the young girl's responses and wonder how and why a parent would allow this. Let's stick with the unnamed boy.

Would a young boy tell a reporter to keep his name out of the paper, or would a parent do that? The answer was obvious. So, why did the girl's parents allow her name to be listed?

Something smelled off.

But here was a young girl, apparently one of Renee's best friends, leading the entire article. Renee's last act was to deliver strawberries to a neighbor.

To this girl? To someone else?

No matter how hard I tried, I couldn't get over the article's tone. Why had the reporter given this young girl so much power?

I didn't like the piece for various reasons. Maybe it was indicative of the times. Perhaps this was a standard practice in 1977, and parents trusted reporters to chat with their children about adult matters. But to interview kids about the murder of Renee? Why hadn't the reporter asked parents for comments?

I wondered if I was reading into things and making up stories out of nothing. Probably. Even though I wasn't getting any closer to the truth, I knew it was healthy to do one thing: Question everything.

Why had the star of the article's parents allowed this, though? None of her quotes were helpful to the investigation.

I had to find out why she spoke to the press and if she was a group member yet.

More importantly, I had to see if she was still alive.

ALIVE AND WELL

As if the stars aligned, the star of the Hartford Courant article joined our Facebook group! As I did every evening, I scrolled through the posts and read everyone's latest comments.

In a post that recommended interviewing the neighborhood children with whom Renee was to play with that tragic night, the star of the article, now an adult, posted the following comment:

"Yes, I was that friend, her death has haunted me for years. I think about Renee often even named 1 of my children (middle name) after her. Would have been first name but jerk husband at the time!"

But it was her only one.

A few days after the comment, I sent her the following email:

Dear _____,

Thanks for joining our group! I review the feed once a week, so I appreciate you having the courage to leave a comment like that. It's touching that you have honored Renee's memory with one of your children. That first husband sounds like no peach, though. Just kidding! In all seriousness, would you be up for a phone chat? I just wanted to get clarity on a few things that will help shape the accuracy of my future book. No rush on replying. Thanks again.

To this day, it still says SENT.

Could she not see it unless we were Facebook buddies, or was she avoiding me?

I hoped it was the former.

I wanted to respect silence in this type of situation. But if a few of Renee's best friends were willing to chat with me, why wasn't this one doing so? Why hadn't I received a simple rejection? Was it just too hard for her to go there emotionally?

THE BURDEN OF PATHOS

A group member named Lisa Victoria was related to Renee Freer. She had a passion and an enthusiasm that was desperately needed. One post in particular made my skin crawl. It read:

How can anyone live their life knowing they killed a beautiful little girl in such a brutal manner? How could they look her in the eyes then smash her beautiful face and live with that image knowing that was the very last thing Renee ever saw and would see nothing ever again? How could the family and/or friends of this suspect continue to live their lives as if nothing ever happened? How would they all feel if that was their daughter or granddaughter laying there in the woods murdered? How would they feel if the last thing their daughter or granddaughter saw was the face of a cold-blooded killer with a rock aimed at her face? How does anyone that has information not come forward? How??? It's been 47 years, please let Renee, her mom, and her grandparents RIP. It's not fair you are living your life, celebrating milestones, and going about your life as if nothing happened. How do you do that? Renee has not been forgotten by those who cared about her and her short life! I pray you have lived a tortured life!!! I pray that when you close your eyes at night to go to sleep you still see Renee's eyes taking their last look of life as you killed her brutally. But believe it or not I don't wish what was done to Renee to be done to your child. Be thankful!

I admired Lisa Victoria for having the guts to post something like this. Furthermore, the last line told me what kind of person she was. But I knew a post like this would only land with some of the group members. I knew that no amount of pathos in a Facebook post would make the killer crack.

They had to be broken down in a different manner.

GROUNDSWELL

The group members started doing their own thing, and it excited me.

A visual artist designed a flyer for free!

Another member suggested a QR code go on it so people could join the group from their phones.

Some members wanted to give money towards hiring a private investigator.

Others complained to the police or the state attorney's office. I may have encouraged a few members to do this. (Sorry, not sorry, Monroe Police).

Various people hung the created flyers around random towns, pissing off locals in the towns of Seymour and Southbury. It made everyone wonder why those townsfolk were so annoyed. Perhaps someone close to the killer lived in one of those towns. It seemed like a long shot.

Masuk High School was willing to discuss creating a scholarship in Renee Freer's name.

A brewery near Monroe wanted to assist in any way they could.

The positive energy excited me to no end. Often labeled grumpy and somewhat negative, I knew there was no room for apathy or negativity. There was only room for positivity and old-school persistence.

If a positive result was to be had, the community of Monroe had to unite and apply pressure all over the state. This sort of effort would help the cops because it would keep the case alive in the people's minds connected to the crime.

THE NEW ADMINISTRATOR

Rick Canfield Jr. was my brother from another mother. We had been close since attending St. Jude in the first grade. I had a traumatic Kindergarten experience at Fawn Hollow, so my mother made me attend the school overpopulated with nuns. I couldn't speak to why Rick attended. But during a service where the pastor announced yet another local death, Rick became sick and barfed. I distinctly remember seeing a pink substance on the floor. My mother, a substitute teacher, snapped into action and cared for him. We have been friends ever since.

As an adult, Rick wasn't the weakling I met at Saint Jude. He had turned into this monster of a presence. He has Italian and Native American in his blood. The dude looks like he could have taken down Custer's army all by himself. I had reservations about getting him involved with the project because I thought there was a chance he would find out who committed the murder, yank them out of their house, and drag them to the Monroe Police station. He's got a "crazy switch," and I don't like to be the one that sets it off. He's got a survivor instinct that I don't possess. He is the type that could survive in the South African bush with a dollar, a bottle of water, and a small knife.

If something happened to me for writing this book, I knew he would move heaven and earth to lock up everyone responsible. Or worse. He was a part-time researcher, part-time confidence coach, part-time debater, and full-time maniac.

He was connected to people from the time. I was connected to Ken Heim.

It felt like Renee brought us together again.

To make us even better friends? Or because her spirit knew we were bold and persistent enough to go for it?

I was just a writer, but Rick was a maniac, and I needed a few of those in my camp.

I always laughed at his random lines. "Don't piss on my back, and tell me it's raining, okay!" Or when he would research some information and pivot to a different thought. He would say, "Right church. Wrong pew."

I was fortunate to have his involvement, even if his findings or opinions didn't make it into my book. His brain didn't work like most people. Having someone like him sift through the information I had access to would keep me fresh and allow for regular debates to occur.

Cocky bastard he was, he joked, "I need the police reports. Just for one day! Just one, and I would have this thing solved." I playfully agreed with him but knew that the cops had their hands full with a case that could change the legacy of their careers.

They had to move like a snail; we could move at the speed of a rocket.

Renee's case was way more intricate than I ever imagined. It had to be. There was no other explanation for why securing justice for her would take so long. I reminded Rick about that. But he disagreed. He thought this case was a lot simpler than anyone imagined. Worse than that, he wanted drama. He wanted conflict. While I wanted none of those things, I made him the group administrator because he wanted justice for Renee Freer more than I did, and I didn't think that was possible.

POSSIBLE SCENARIOS

(#1-9)

#1: Renee Freer was bludgeoned to death by John Rice Jr. He went into hiding and never killed another human being.

Very unlikely

#2: A total stranger entered the neighborhood and bludgeoned Renee Freer to death. The stranger had no ties to her or anyone in the family. It was just a random moment of opportunity.

Very unlikely

#3: A male teenager in the neighborhood bludgeoned Renee Freer to death. He hid whatever evidence he could. He lied to his friends, family, and everyone since that day. He is the only one who knows about it.

Unlikely

#4: A male teenager in the neighborhood bludgeoned Renee Freer to death. After cutting through the woods and hiding at a friend's house, he informed his parents about what he did, and they snapped into action to cover it up. They used a member of the press or a vulnerable person in the police department to shift the attention away from their son. No one paid for the crime. No one felt guilty.

Unlikely

#5: A male teenager in the neighborhood bludgeoned Renee Freer to death. He informed his parents, and they snapped into action to cover up whatever they could. After questioning, the family remained in town to make it look like there was nothing to hide, yet they had been hiding in plain sight all along.

More Likely Than Not

#6: A girl in the neighborhood bludgeoned Renee Freer to death. Her family members were so shocked that she did it that they snapped into action to cover up what she did. She, along with her siblings, pretended to know nothing. The whole incident amused her while it tortured her family forever.

More Likely Than Not

#7: A male teenager in the neighborhood struck Renee Freer with a large stone after failing to molest her. He informed his father, who arrived on the scene and finished the job with the kill shot. This caused a permanent rift within the family. They lived with the guilt of knowing all along but knew that remaining silent was their only way to go. No one paid for the crime. Some in the family felt guilty. Just not enough to have the guts to say something to the cops.

More Likely Than Not

#8: A male teenager in the neighborhood bludgeoned Renee Freer to death after a game (tag, doctor, kill the carrier) got out of hand. He hid whatever evidence he could. He arrived at the one of the nearby Chalk Hill graduation parties to create an alibi but told his family the truth because he had to. They helped cover up his crime and started a nasty rumor about a family that lived near Williams Drive. The rumor stuck and nearly ruined said family's life.

Likely

#9: A male teenager in the neighborhood bludgeoned Renee Freer to death because she was pure and innocent while he was suffering inside an abusive environment. He informed his parents, and they snapped into action to cover up whatever they could. After questioning and some months passed, the family left town and was able to keep the cops away because there was a lack of evidence. They knew it because, aside from the rock, they hid or burned any other evidence. No one paid for the crime. A sibling or two felt somewhat guilty.

Very Likely

THE REAL COWARDS

My brain was able to process how a disturbed teenager, male or female, could do this to a young girl.

But my brain couldn't process how a parent would cover it up.

No 13-year-old could keep this lie without having the parents as a buffer.

No way.

The teen could have been dragged to jail, served their time in juvie, and after a few short years (because they would be brief), walked out having learned the greatest lesson of their life.

But no.

FATHERS

Ken Heim lost his father at 16.

Even though my father lived until 2020, I hadn't seen him since 1990.

Greg, the friend I almost murdered, lost his father at a young age.

What did any of this mean?

There's a certain stability that a father should bring with his presence. But I have also been around some characters in my day, making me think that having a fierce and protective mother was all a child needed.

The teammate's father that would cuss him out endlessly for missing a pitch or making an error in the outfield.

The former friend's father who expected his dinner to be hot and ready the second he entered the main floor, and once he sat, the very second he sat, he would belt out asinine and hurtful questions like, "What the hell is this shit?!" He kept his wife in tow by making her a willing servant. It didn't matter that he embarrassed her in front of her children's friends.

I pried out many letters and pictures from a manila envelope and studied all of them. My father, a legendary abuser of alcohol, had written down a list that highlighted his reasons for relapses.

1) *He signed up for the US Army in 1965. As he was getting ready to leave for Fort Dix, New Jersey, his mother talked him out of it. He "felt like a coward."*

2) *His wife (and my mother) might have been unfaithful. He protects her character by suggesting that these could be perceptions instead of truths.*

3) *He divorced my mother in 1986 and abandoned his children.*

"These are the most painful incidents in my life and caused me to behave improperly, including drug abuse and drinking to excess."

I appreciated the straightforward honesty of my father's thoughts. Notable omissions, however, were these: stating how much he cared for his children and neglecting how often he beat the living shit out of my mother and brother.

He could express the guilt on paper but couldn't do so in reality, not even when death came calling.

It scared me that internal wishes could remain inside of someone for so long. That's when I realized that the person who killed Renee Freer would never see the light and own this crime. Waiting for them to confess on a deathbed was fool's gold.

I never thought an adult committed the murder.

I frequently thought a father dictated the aftermath of how this crime played out because his son or daughter did something evil, yes. And when fathers have things to lose (control, status, respect), they do what is necessary, even if it means covering up the murder of an innocent girl.

I went to sleep, trying to find the perfect position. I reflected positively on my times with Ken and the one question he asked me that still rang in my ears. "Erik, was I ever mean to you?" My answer was an emphatic no. While it made me feel good to tell him that, it also made me reflect on the question and connect it to what I thought happened here.

Was a father mean to his children? Had he learned what happened to Renee and covered it up? Had he ordered his wife, kids, and neighbors to shut their fucking mouths? Had he tried to buy off a cop or, at the very least, dictate when and for how long the cops could interview his kids? This scenario felt much closer to the truth than a boogeyman terrorizing a cul-de-sac and vanishing into thin air.

Fathers, man. They have the power to ruin so much in their path. But not Ken Heim. He was a good one. And he would have turned me in had I blown my best friend's brains all over his wall of snacks. I couldn't say the same about my biological father, though. I didn't know much, but I knew this: He never would have let me ruin *his* life.

I FEEL SORRY FOR YOU. SORT OF.

I hearkened back to the time I almost killed my best friend.

And I wondered what would have happened if that bullet had penetrated Greg's face.

Would I have remained frozen in fear while the blood poured out of his deformed head?

Would I have grabbed him by the ankles, discarded his body in the woods, and tried to clean up before my mother or stepfather was the wiser?

Would I have lied and said he went missing or that we had an argument and he walked home?

Would my stepfather have participated in selling a lie so I could maintain my freedom?

The answer is no. My mother and stepfather would have tossed my ass into the back of the car and taken me to the police station. My mother would have ordered me to take ownership and willingly accept my fate in juvie.

But the adults in the Freer equation denied the killer of the chance to take responsibility. They denied him the opportunity to atone for his foolish sin. And in so doing, they devalued the acceptance of wrongdoing. They stunted the killer's growth and asked other family members connected to the situation to keep the lie a secret for years.

That is unforgivable.

You are not to blame for that.

You made a stupid decision that any teen boy could make.

But you had no role models.

You needed guidance.

You, essentially, had no parents.

And I feel sorry for you.

Giggles shouldn't. But I do. Even if you killed Renee Freer to see what it was like. It wasn't your fault that you didn't value the existence of others. That's on your parents and only them.

THE NEIGHBORHOOD KIDDOS

Spared from dealing with the National Archives, a helpful citizen relied on a land trust to provide the names of homeowners, renters, and their kids in the area at that time. They sent me the following names of kiddos from Williams Drive, Birchwood, and Hattertown Road: Harold Scully, Carol Pekar, Cynthia Campos, Anthony Campos, Glen Johnson, Laurie Johnson, Fabio Pawlus, Claudio Pawlus, Julie Zullo, Mark Zullo, Jeff Meeker, Pamela Meeker, Susan Meeker, John Maiorino, Bonnie Maiorino, Ray Maiorino, Lyssa Mitchell, Gregory Levan, Wayne Horgan, Chris Lowry, Andria Lowry, Rich Lowry, Bruce Schwab, Corinne Schwab, Robby Schwab, Joe Lowden, John Crone, and Debbie Crone.

I dragged my finger up and down the list, knowing that some of these people were members of the WHO KILLED RENEE FREER group. It would be easy to target those who didn't join and speculate that their absence carried major significance, but some, especially those in their 60s, didn't use social media much. Most of these people likely had no connection to Renee besides living nearby or occasionally playing in each other's neighborhoods. But one or more of them had a strong connection to her, and that needed to be pushed and explored to the nth degree.

I knew I hadn't solved anything. And since I didn't have access to the files of an active police investigation, I wondered if any of these people had spoken to the police and if they had become persons of interest.

That's the funny thing about murder mysteries. The prime suspect could be any of the people on the list (assuming it's 100% accurate), or it could be someone as random as John Rice Jr. sweeping in and out of small towns to do his bidding.

One thing was for sure: Renee knew who attacked her and who witnessed it. But all because of getting a bad hand (hospital autopsy instead of a forensic one), the person responsible and the people who knew more than they will ever let on have lived their lives like silent cowards.

They had boyfriends and girlfriends. They had children and grandchildren. They had careers and went on vacations. They got to do things as simple as mini golf, karaoke, etc. They got a chance at a whole life because they had no problem being and staying evil.

But maybe Renee wouldn't be as surprised by the murderer as we all assume. Perhaps she would be more surprised that there were a handful in the community who would deny her justice.

Will the killer ever put it in writing? Leave it in an envelope not to be opened until their death? Can the coward do that much?

Short of a confession or the witnesses cracking, I found the situation rather hopeless.

But I knew I wouldn't quit.

Because I still couldn't fathom how someone could have done this to a young girl, I tortured myself by studying the class picture of Renee's class. More than anyone, she is the standout. With her hair. Her outfit. Her beaming smile.

I wanted to print up the pic, cut out Renee's face, and staple it to the foreheads of all those who knew what happened. Live with and be reminded of it daily. It is your Scarlet Letter.

No one would smile like that if they thought evil was in the world. No one would smile like that, knowing a so-called friend betrayed her. No one would smile like that, knowing that someone close bashed her head in on the eve of finishing third grade and abandoned her in the woods like she was absolutely worthless.

THE TEDDY

A member of the Facebook group commented that Renee would have gotten justice had her body not been buried with a teddy bear. I hated the statement's implication because it made me wonder if this person was criticizing Renee's parents for making such a heartfelt gesture. But then it became clear that there was a bite mark under her breast, which changed everything. Since members of the group reacted hostilely to the user's comment, I contacted Stephen Biley, the former cop, to see if there was any truth to it. "That is a fact. You can quote me on that. I don't give a shit. Henry Lee and Jack Solomon went through the, uh, autopsy report and came up with a semi-lunar mark that was in the report, and that's what resulted in getting the exhumation order to bring her out of the ground and then when we got her out of the ground, they opened it up, we scraped off the dead skin and where the teddy bear was, was a mark and we couldn't get a picture of the semi-lunar mark because it was gone."

So, there it was. It wasn't that a cop or firefighter made an error at Renee's crime scene; this seemed to imply that someone missed this specific mark on her body during her hospital autopsy.

No wonder the current regime at the Monroe Police Department had their hands full. How do they solve a crime after someone missed the one clue that could have ended the case? News flash: They couldn't.

ONE OF THE ACCUSED

Two teens' names kept coming up when I would ask people who they thought killed Renee.

They had to be differentiated by their last name since they shared the same first name.

Like a fisherman trying to bait his targets, I made contact with a new member on Facebook that was close to one of the male teens. While I was thrilled to learn about hangout sessions from the late 70s, I couldn't help but wonder: Will one of the principal persons of interest speak with me? Will they spin a yarn declaring their innocence? Will they refuse to talk, thus creating more attention and intrigue around their name? Will they "out" the guilty party after all these years?

I had to be patient. But it was tough to be patient, knowing there was a chance, albeit slim, that one of the alleged killers would speak with me. That is, of course, if this old buddy could convince them to do so.

In the meantime, I familiarized myself with the music of The Grateful Dead. A hater of pot and loafing around, I couldn't believe how much I started to like their music. Maybe the deadhead gods would be on my side.

GOOGLE EARTH

(Part Two)

Weeks passed, and I wasn't getting responses from the so-called friends of one of the primary persons of interest in Renee's murder. After consuming three IPAs and a shot of whiskey, I visited their profile. It was active again; they were regularly making posts. Motivated by alcohol or impatience, I typed the following note:

Dear ____,

I am writing a book about the Renee Freer murder that happened in 1977. I am almost done with the book. A few in the town said that cops worked you pretty hard on that one. If you were willing to chat for 5-10 minutes, it would be great. Use my book to clear your name and narrow this thing down. While your name came up occasionally, most told me they didn't think it was you. If you want it, take this opportunity. I'll ask a few questions free of judgment. I do not want to resurrect memories from a tough time. But this is gaining momentum way beyond my book. There is a FB group and IG page. People are hanging flyers in random towns. Events are lined up for 2025. I just would want to put an end to *this for you. I sincerely swear that I would cancel every event if the person that did it came forward. Hope to hear from you. Happy Almost 4th. – E.C. Hanson*

Even though I had consumed a few drinks, I knew there wasn't a false note in my message. Were their events planned? Yes. A book launch at a gifts and collectibles store in Shelton. Three library events (Oxford, Monroe, and Woodbury). A brewery event in Oxford. A discussion at Sacred Heart University's Criminal Justice program. An episode on Kristen Seavey's popular podcast called *Murder, She Told*. Did I sincerely want them to clear their name? Yes, because I wasn't convinced they killed Renee. And I had a strange feeling that this case would get more attention in the coming years, and everyone's assumptions about Renee's murder would eat up the community I was raised in. If they explained how and why they couldn't have committed the murder, people from the time would know exactly who did. Like Voldemort, it was a name people seemed to be afraid to say out loud. And as my friend Rick said, everyone needed to start normalizing it. I knew that this could and would happen if the other contender worked up the nerve to chat with me. Even if it was for a few minutes.

Unfortunately, they never did.

Despite some of their high school friends insisting that they were cleared, I never removed them from my list due to their longstanding friendship with the son of one of the cops who worked the case. A friendship, by the way, that some Monroe cops weren't ever aware of.

FLOODGATES

Because I got the impression people were terrified of reprisal from the killer, I created a post in the Facebook group, and I invited members who were around for Renee's horrific murder to share who they thought was responsible.

Once they discovered that it *wasn't* a mentally challenged boy, a member from the Schwab family, the one pictured on Google Earth, or John Rice Jr., there was a unanimous verdict on who it had to be. Keeping them anonymous for safety reasons, their responses about a thirteen or fourteen-year-old male got my attention.

Anonymous Person #1 - "He was not a nice guy."

Anonymous Person #2 - "He was known to have a short temper."

Anonymous Person #3 - "He was aggressive at times."

Anonymous Person #4 - "He liked to play head games."

Anonymous Person #5 - "He always had a wild look in his eye."

Anonymous Person #6 - "He loved to fight."

Anonymous Person #7 - "He thought nothing about punching somebody just for the heck of it."

Anonymous Person #8 - "He beat up my friend for no reason at all."

Anonymous Person #9 - "The girls he grabbed inappropriately and insisted they were his girlfriends."

Anonymous Person #10 - "He had intimate knowledge of Renee and who her closest neighborhood friends were."

Anonymous Person #11 - "(Mr. Google Earth) was afraid of him."

Well, well, well. It spoke volumes if the other person of interest was scared of this particular male teen. But what landed more was when a person from the time shared this: "He lived in close proximity to Renee."

If that was the case, people from the time familiar with the dead end road could quickly narrow this one down if the above observations matched theirs. And if they never had considered this particular male, perhaps it was time to contact the Monroe Police.

But what did I know? I wasn't there for the big event. I wasn't a detective, reporter, or private investigator. I was just a dude who watched too many episodes of *Dateline* and *See No Evil*.

A BULLSHIT ARGUMENT

A bullshit argument went around from those connected to the main persons of interest, and, quite frankly, I was sick and tired of hearing it. The paraphrased argument was this: But he has kids and grandkids! There is no way in the world he could have done something like that!

But both of the main persons of interest had kids and grandkids, so one of them, the guilty party, defeated the argument's merits. This wasn't a boogeyman from New Canaan. It was a male teen from Monroe who smashed Renee's head several inches into the ground. I repeat: several inches into the fucking ground.

Not wanting to know more about the crime but needing to, Stephen Biley, the first officer to the scene, said, "She had no face."

So, which family man do you think was capable of such rage? The one that was a tad peculiar or the one that lived close to Renee and had a penchant for bullying everyone he came across?

LIKE A DRUM

I traveled back to that day when I almost shot Greg in the head. And like you, whoever did this, I would have lied to my parents, his mother and sisters. I would have tried to hide the lie for as long as I possibly could, but there would come a day when I would crack. I know it. There wouldn't be enough booze or drugs on the planet to help me forget. It would always be there. Beating and beating.

You can hear Renee's name over and over and still not crack?

You really can?

Renee. Freer.

Renee. Freer.

Renee. Freer.

Renee. Freer.

Still nothing?

Renee. Freer.

Renee. Freer.

Is that it? You're dead inside?

Renee might be gone, but her spirit has resurrected the town of Monroe. Renee is watching and waiting, and Monroe is watching and waiting.

They're both waiting for you to do the right thing.

Will you do the right thing?

Do you have the courage to do the right thing?

I repeat: Do you have the courage to do the right thing?

Renee. Freer.

Renee. Freer.

Renee. Freer.

Renee. Freer.

Renee. Freer.

Renee. Freer.

Renee. Freer.

Renee. Freer.

How long can you deny her justice?

Renee. Freer.

Renee. Freer.

Renee. Freer.

Renee. Freer.

How long can you threaten your loved ones to remain quiet?

Renee. Freer.

Renee. Freer.

Renee. Freer.

Renee. Freer.

It will never stop.

In between the crickets chirping or after the frog's ribbits...

Renee. Freer.

Renee. Freer.

When the water from the shower hits your skull...

Renee. Freer.

After your alarm beeps.

Renee. Freer.

While you're stuck in traffic.

Renee. Freer.

Renee. Freer.

When your siblings look at you sideways.

Renee. Freer.

Renee. Freer.

When your siblings ignore your calls or texts.

Renee. Freer.

Renee. Freer.

While you hunt or fish or hike through the woods.

Renee. Freer.

Renee. Freer.

When you crush a can of beer.

Renee. Freer.

When you toss back a nip of hard liquor.

Renee. Freer.

Renee. Freer.

When you kiss your wife at night.

Renee. Freer.

Renee. Freer.

When someone laughs and it reminds you that they called her Giggles.

Renee. Freer.

Renee. Freer.

When you blast some Grateful Dead or Scorpions or Judas Priest or Kiss or AC/DC or Journey or Van Halen to drown out your self-created pain...

Renee. Freer.

Renee. Freer.

When you consider taking ownership and find a reason not to do one right thing in your life...

Renee. Freer.

Renee. Freer.

When you visit and hang with the friends and family that have carried this huge lie for you.

Renee. Freer.

Renee. Freer.

When someone came forward in the 90s with new information and you somehow slipped through the cracks...

Renee. Freer.

Renee. Freer.

When you attend a loved one's funeral and have to secretly acknowledge that you put a beautiful girl in a coffin...

Renee. Freer.

Renee. Freer.

When there is a power outage, and you must rely on candles and silence to get you by...

Renee. Freer.

Renee. Freer.

When you brush your teeth...

Renee. Freer.

Renee. Freer.

While you wonder what will happen when new people discover your identity...

Renee. Freer.

Renee. Freer.

You happily signed up for this torture. You will never stop hearing her name over and over and over again unless…

Unless…

…unless…

You come forward and confess.

If you're too afraid to do that (telling the truth is scarier than committing murder, I guess), write down what you did with the order of "SEND TO THE MONROE POLICE DEPARTMENT AFTER I DIE."

Those are your two options.

You're man enough to kill a girl under the age of ten. Are you brave enough to surrender? Are you caring enough to give closure to a still grieving family and allow your family members to stop carrying the monumental weight of your disgusting lie?

If not, the devil is waiting for you.

And his arms are held out wide.

Even he is saying what you don't want to hear.

Renee. Freer.

Renee. Freer.

Renee. Freer.

Renee. Freer.

Renee. Freer.

Renee. Freer.

Renee. Freer.

Renee. Freer.

Renee. Freer.

Renee. Freer.

Renee. Freer.

Renee. Freer.

Renee. Freer.

Renee. Freer.
Renee. Freer.
Renee. Freer.
Renee. Freer.
Renee. Freer.
Renee. Freer.
Renee. Freer.
Renee. Freer.
Renee. Freer.
Renee. Freer.

EPILOGUE

I returned to the cabin I shared with my former stepfather and two stepsisters. I drove down the wishbone driveway, marveling that I was returning to a place I never expected to see again.

I tried to ignore the fact that a user named *trshy_panda* in the newly formed Instagram group had been referring to Renee as "worm food" and then claiming they smashed her face in. I knew it was likely to be a troll since the account was public instead of private, but I also wondered if someone connected to the killer would be this stupid. I wouldn't rule it out. Narcissistic personalities couldn't resist reminding people of their power. I couldn't tell you what would happen to such a user, but I couldn't be bothered by it. I couldn't even worry that the case was still unsolved since I only studied it for a few months. I was optimistic, though. But I shifted my focus to the moment at hand because I had a reunion to experience. Unfortunately, my former stepsisters wouldn't be present.

What would it be like to see Ken again?

I had no clue, but I knew all this was about to happen because of Renee Freer. The only way for me to repay her was to never quit on her and to remind the general public that a coward killed her, and his family chose silence over giving her surviving relatives justice.

ACKNOWLEDGMENTS

I want to thank Rick Canfield, Bill Bittar, Eric Giordano, Mark Towse, Mardi Kane, Norman Rancourt, Tony Anuci, Dane Hanson, my former stepfather and his daughters, and (nearly) every person who joined the Facebook group devoted to Renee's case. If this case ever gets solved, it will be because of your collective energy.

And even though those currently working for the Monroe Police Department couldn't help me in any way with this book, they never discouraged me from writing it. That could only mean we shared a common goal: much-needed justice for Renee Freer.

BIBLIOGRAPHY ARTICLES:

Bittar, Bill. "Author pursues book to shine spotlight on Monroe's only unsolved murder." The Monroe Sun (April 14, 2024).

Bittar, Bill. "Monroe police urge Renee Freer's killer to come forward." The Monroe Sun (April 18, 2024).

Bittar, Bill. "Online sleuths hope posters turn up heat on Renee Freer's killer." The Monroe Sun (July 7, 2024).

Bowser, Jacqueline. "The Boogeyman." News and Clues (May 19, 2016).

Mutchler, Kayla. "Monroe's unsolved child murder: An author looks to shed new light on Renee Freer's cold case." Connecticut Post (April 19, 2024).

"Innocence Stolen Forever." Savagewatch – Unsolved Crime.

"Murder of Rene Freer." Counteverymystery.blogspot.com (November 1, 2017).

"Police Quiz 'Several' In Monroe Girl's Slaying." The Bridgeport Post (June 24, 1977).

"POLICE HOPE DNA TEST WILL HELP SOLVE 22-YEAR-OLD MURDER CASE." The Hartford Courant (July 7, 1999).

Smith, J. Herbert. "Bludgeoning of Girl is Mystery." The Hartford Courant (June 24, 1977).

WEBSITES:

change.org

courant.com

earth.google.com

facebook.com

hickcoxfuneralhome.com

newspapers.com

reddit.com

foia.gov

othram.com

portal.ct.gov/ocme

portal.ct.gov/ocme

Justice.gov

Hannibal show – "Antipasto" episode

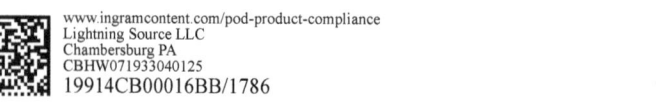